**Stepping into Standards
Theme Series**

Going Buggy!

Written by
Kimberly Jordano and Tebra Corcoran

Editor: Teri L. Fisch
Illustrator: Darcy Tom
Cover Illustrator: Kimberly Schamber
Designer: Moonhee Pak
Cover Designer: Moonhee Pak
Art Director: Tom Cochrane
Project Director: Carolea Williams

Table of Contents

Introduction

Due to the often-changing national, state, and district standards, it is often difficult to "squeeze in" fascinating topics for student enrichment on top of meeting required standards and including a balanced program in your classroom curriculum. The *Stepping into Standards Theme Series* will help you incorporate required subjects and skills for your kindergarten and first-grade children while engaging them in a fun theme. Children will participate in a variety of language arts experiences to help them with **phonemic awareness** and **reading** and **writing** skills. They will also have fun with **math activities, hands-on science activities,** and **social studies class projects.**

The creative lessons in *Going Buggy!* provide imaginative, innovative ideas to help you motivate children as you turn your classroom into a garden filled with bugs. The activities will inspire children to explore bugs as well as provide them with opportunities to enhance their knowledge and meet standards.

Invite children to explore a garden of bugs as they
- participate in phonemic awareness activities that feature theme-related poems
- create mini-books that reinforce guided reading and sight word practice
- contribute to shared and independent reading and writing experiences about bugs
- practice measuring a flower with a caterpillar
- learn about, observe, and draw parts of a bug
- explore kindness and respect for all living things
- complete several fun art projects as they turn their room into a garden of bugs
- participate in a Bug Bonanza to showcase their work

Each resource book in the *Stepping into Standards Theme Series* includes standards information, easy-to-use reproducibles, and a full-color overhead transparency to help you integrate a fun theme into your required curriculum. You will see how easy it can be to incorporate creative activities with academic requirements while children enjoy their exploration of bugs!

Meeting Standards

Language Arts

	Old Black Fly Alphabet Book, page 7	This Little Bug, page 8	Rhyming Bugs, page 8	Reading Aloud, page 12	Morning Message, page 13	Pocket Chart Stories, page 14	Sentence Puzzle, page 14	Giant Bugs, Little Bugs mini-book, page 16	A Spider on Me! mini-book, page 20	Swat That Bug at Home!, page 24	A Butterfly Birthday Party, page 26	A "Webby" Word Wall, page 30	Bug Hunting, page 31	Fantastic Fly Facts, page 32	Yuck! No!, page 33	I'm as Quick as a . . ., page 34	A Baggy Full of Bugs, page 35	Rhyming Bees, page 37	Fantastic Fireflies, page 38
Phonemic Awareness																			
Identify beginning consonant sounds	●	●																	
Identify letters	●																		
Identify rhyming words			●															●	
Isolate beginning sounds	●	●																	
Recognize rhythm and rhyme		●	●															●	●
Substitute beginning consonant sounds			●																
Reading																			
Apply phonics concepts	●							●	●	●	●	●				●			●
Apply reading strategies	●				●	●	●	●	●	●	●					●			
Develop awareness of concepts of print					●	●	●	●	●	●	●	●	●	●	●	●			
Develop oral language skills	●	●	●		●	●	●	●	●	●	●	●	●	●					
Identify plot, characters, conflict, and resolution					●														
Improve reading comprehension						●	●	●											
Improve reading fluency								●	●	●	●	●	●	●	●				●
Improve story comprehension	●				●			●	●					●	●	●	●		●
Make predictions					●														
Recognize sight word vocabulary	●				●	●	●	●	●	●	●	●	●	●	●	●	●	●	
Track words from left to right					●	●	●	●	●	●	●	●	●	●	●	●	●		
Writing																			
Apply phonics skills					●			●	●	●		●	●	●	●	●	●	●	●
Brainstorm and organize ideas	●											●	●	●	●		●		
Choose correct punctuation					●										●	●	●		
Follow spelling rules					●			●	●	●		●	●	●	●	●	●	●	●
Incorporate letter and word spacing					●						●	●	●	●	●	●	●	●	●
Model letter formation					●							●	●			●		●	
Model sentence structure					●										●	●			
Practice correct letter formation					●			●	●	●			●	●	●	●	●	●	●
Write complete sentences															●	●	●		

Meeting Standards

Math
Science
Social Studies

Standard	Caterpillar Inches, page 40	The Buggy Backpack, page 41	Ladybug Clock, page 41	How Many Bugs?, page 45	Buzzing Bugs Glyph, page 46	Caterpillar Film Canisters, page 48	Colorful Bug Pie Graph, page 49	Bug Observation Box, page 50	Bug Body Puzzles, page 50	When I Try . . ., page 54	Don't Step on the Ants!, page 56	Bug Bonanza, page 58	Beautiful Butterflies, page 58	Spider Bulletin Board Graph, page 59	Bug Treats, page 60	Bug Box Café, page 60	Flyswatter Reading Sticks, page 60
Math																	
Add				•											•		
Analyze data					•		•							•			
Count		•		•	•	•									•		
Count using one-to-one correspondence		•		•	•	•									•		
Make a graph							•							•			
Make patterns	•	•										•	•				
Measure length	•																
Sequence events						•											
Skip count		•															
Sort by attributes		•															
Tell time			•														
Understand number families				•													
Use fractions to represent data							•										
Write numbers correctly	•			•			•								•		
Science																	
Identify bug anatomy									•								
Make observations							•	•									
Record observations daily								•									
Understand bug life cycles													•				
Understand how bugs' physical traits help them survive							•	•									
Social Studies																	
Build self-esteem											•		•				
Explore kindness												•					
Practice being considerate												•					
Understand the importance of perseverance											•						
Additional Language Arts																	
Apply reading strategies		•								•	•				•		•
Develop oral language skills					•	•	•			•	•		•		•	•	•
Follow spelling rules	•				•	•	•			•	•	•			•		
Follow step-by-step directions				•	•									•		•	
Improve story comprehension	•	•	•	•		•				•	•		•	•			
Incorporate letter and word spacing	•				•	•	•			•	•		•		•		
Model letter formation							•				•				•		
Practice correct letter formation	•					•				•	•	•	•		•		

Instant Learning Environment

This resource includes a full-color overhead transparency of a garden environment that can be used in a variety of ways to enhance the overall theme of the unit and make learning more interactive. Simply place the transparency on an overhead projector, and shine it against a blank wall, white butcher paper, or a white sheet. Then, choose an idea from the list below, or create your own ideas for using this colorful backdrop.

Unit Introduciton

Give children clues about the bugs unit. For example, say *We are going to study about a type of animal. These animals are small. They have three body parts.* Invite children to use the clues to discuss what the unit might be about. Then, display the transparency to give children a quick overview of the garden environment and an introduction to the unit.

Or, cut out puzzle pieces from an 8½" x 11" (21.5 cm x 28 cm) sheet of paper. Place the puzzle pieces on top of the transparency on the overhead projector so they cover it entirely. Turn on the projector. None of the garden environment will show. Remove one puzzle piece at a time, and describe the uncovered section. Invite children to identify the environment. Then, continue to remove pieces, asking children to predict what they might see next until you have revealed the entire transparency.

Dramatic Play

Use the transparency as a backdrop for children to perform the dramatic play described on page 26. Have children wear a character headband (glue cutouts from the Bug Props reproducibles on pages 28–29 to sentence strips) as they perform.

Bugs in a Garden Mural

Make a mural. Project the transparency on a piece of white butcher paper. Have children trace the scene and paint it. Encourage children to draw additional objects or glue construction paper bugs on the mural. Have children practice spelling bug-related words by writing the names of creatures and objects (e.g., caterpillar, wings) on the mural.

Phonemic Awareness

ABC

Old Black Fly Alphabet Book

MATERIALS

✓ *Old Black Fly* by Jim Aylesworth
✓ letter cutouts (capital and lowercase)
✓ construction paper
✓ plastic flies
✓ art supplies

Read aloud *Old Black Fly*. Point out that it is an alphabet book, and discuss what the fly does and how the words match the letter on each page. Tell children they will create a class alphabet book. As a class, decide where the fly will travel to (e.g., grocery store, toy store, school). Spread out letter cutouts for each letter of the alphabet on a table. Ask each child to choose a matching capital and lowercase cutout and think of an item that begins with that letter that is found in the chosen place (that a fly can land on). For example, if the chosen place is a grocery store, a child can choose the letter C and say *Cc is for catsup*. Show children the book again, and point out how the background on each page was done with splatter painting. Give each child a dark piece of construction paper. Have children use large paintbrushes and a variety of colors of paint to splatter-paint their paper. While the paint is drying, give each child a white piece of construction paper, and have children draw a picture of their item. Give each child a plastic fly, and invite children to glue their fly to their picture. Type the name of each child's item in large bold print, and cut out the words. Glue children's completed picture and typed word to their splatter-painted paper. Have children glue their letter cutouts to their page. Bind children's pages into a class book for independent reading. Write a title (e.g., *Fly Lands in the Grocery Store*) on the cover.

A B C **This Little Bug**

MATERIALS

✓ "This Little Bug" song (page 9)
✓ construction paper

Copy the song "This Little Bug" on construction paper. Sing the song with the class while stressing the beginning sound used in each verse. Choose other bugs, and replace the bolded phonemes and words to continue the song. For example, *This little ladybug sings /l/ songs. It sings /l/ songs all day long. With a* **lick-lack-laddy-lack.** For extra fun, use bug puppets as you sing each verse.

A B C **Rhyming Bugs**

MATERIALS

✓ "What Came Out of the Egg?" poem (page 10)
✓ Bug Cards (page 11)
✓ construction paper
✓ plastic eggs

Copy the poem "What Came Out of the Egg?" on construction paper. Make several copies of the Bug Cards, and cut apart the bugs. Put each bug in a separate plastic egg. (You can put the same bug in many eggs.) Make sure you put a bee in one of the green eggs, an ant in one of the blue eggs, and a fly in one of the yellow eggs. Give each child an egg. Read aloud or sing the poem. As you read about each egg, have children with that color egg open their egg. Invite the child who has a bug that rhymes with the word you said stand up, say the name of his or her bug, and show it to you. To extend the activity, create additional stanzas about different color eggs and rhyming words that match the bugs on the Bug Cards (e.g., *tea* rhymes with *flea*, *materpillar* rhymes with *caterpillar*).

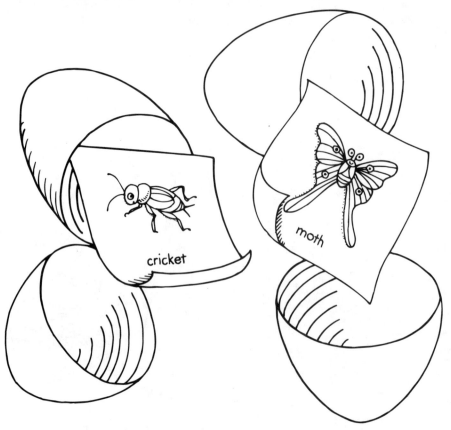

cricket

moth

This Little Bug

(sing to the tune of "This Old Man")

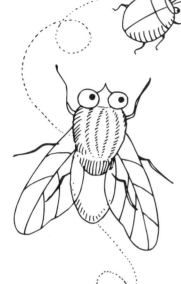

This little bug
Sings /**b**/ songs.
It sings /**b**/ songs all day long.
With a **bick-back-baddy-back**
Sing this buggy song.
It wants you to buzz along.

This little fly
Sings /**f**/ songs.
It sings /**f**/ songs all day long.
With a **fick-fack-faddy-fack**
Sing this buggy song.
It wants you to buzz along.

This little mosquito
Sings /**m**/ songs.
It sings /**m**/ songs all day long.
With a **mick-mack-maddy-mack**
Sing this buggy song.
It wants you to buzz along.

What Came Out of the Egg?

(read to the tune of "Someone's in the Kitchen with Dinah")

What came out of the little green egg?
What came out of the little green egg?
What came out of the little green egg
That rhymes with **tree?**
Bee!

What came out of the little blue egg?
What came out of the little blue egg?
What came out of the little blue egg
That rhymes with **pant?**
Ant!

What came out of the little yellow egg?
What came out of the little yellow egg?
What came out of the little yellow egg
That rhymes with **tie?**
Fly!

Bug Cards

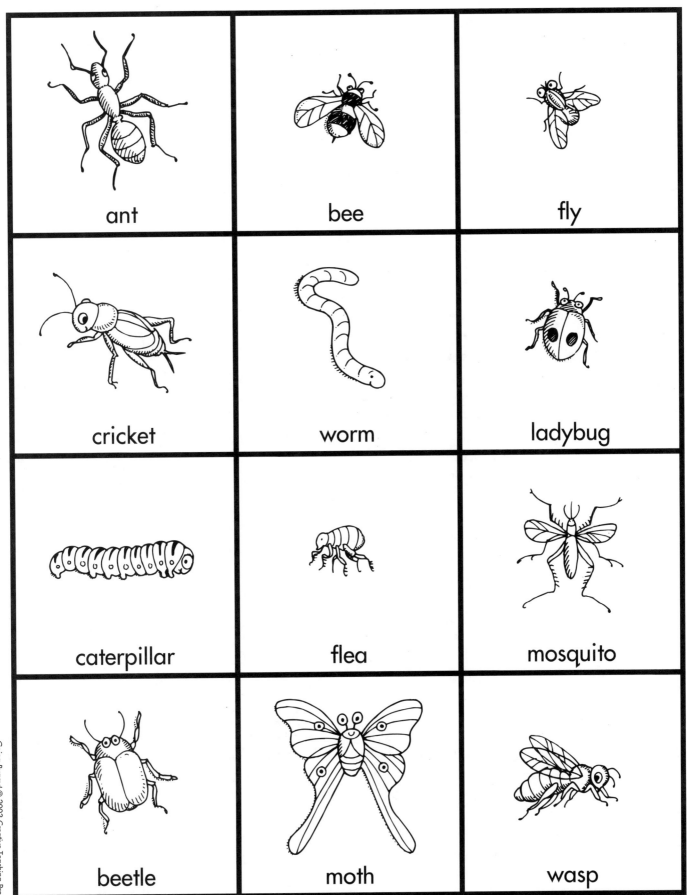

ant	bee	fly
cricket	worm	ladybug
caterpillar	flea	mosquito
beetle	moth	wasp

Modeled Reading

Introduce bugs to your class by reading aloud books from the following literature list or others with similar content. Invite children to look at the book cover and pictures and discuss what they see. Ask them to predict what the book will be about and to point out details that relate to bugs.

Literature List

The Best Bug Parade by Stuart J. Murphy (Econo-Clad Books)

Bugs and Slugs by Judy Tatchell (Usborne Publications)

Bugs! Bugs! Bugs! by Bob Barner (Chronicle Books)

Bugs for Lunch by Margery Facklam (Charlesbridge Publishing)

Charlie the Caterpillar by Dom De Luise (Simon & Schuster)

Creepy Crawlies by Kathryn Kilpatrick (EDC Publications)

The Grouchy Ladybug by Eric Carle (HarperCollins)

Hey, Little Ant by Phillip and Hannah Hoose (Tricycle Press)

The Honeybee and the Robber by Eric Carle (Philomel)

How Many Bugs in a Box? by David Carter (Simon and Schuster)

Icky Bugs Counting Book by Jerry Pallotta (Charlesbridge Publishing)

I'm a Caterpillar by Jean Marzollo (Econo-Clad Books)

I'm as Quick as a Cricket by Audrey Wood (Child's Play)

In the Tall, Tall Grass by Denise Fleming (Henry Holt and Company)

Inch by Inch by Leo Lionni (Econo-Clad Books)

Insects by Robin Bernard (National Geographic Society)

Insects Grow and Change by Elaine Pascoe (Creative Teaching Press)

The Itsy, Bitsy Spider by Iza Trapani (Econo-Clad Books)

Ladybug, Ladybug by Ruth Brown (Dutton)

Miss Spider's Tea Party by David Kirk (Scholastic)

Monarch Butterfly by David M. Schwartz (Creative Teaching Press)

Old Black Fly by Jim Aylesworth (Henry Holt and Company)

The Roly Poly Spider by Jill Sardegna (Scholastic)

Sam and the Firefly by P. D. Eastman (Random House)

Snappy Little Bugs by Claire Nielson and Dug Steer (Silver Dolphin)

Spider on the Floor (Raffi Songs to Read) by Bill Russell (Crown Books)

There Was an Old Lady Who Swallowed a Fly by Pam Adams (Child's Play)

Under One Rock: Bugs, Slugs, and Other Ughs by Anthony D. Fredericks (Dawn Publications)

Underfoot by David M. Schwartz (Creative Teaching Press)

The Very Clumsy Click Beetle by Eric Carle (Philomel)

The Very Hungry Caterpillar by Eric Carle (Philomel)

The Very Lonely Firefly by Eric Carle (Putnam)

Waiting for Wings by Lois Ehlert (Harcourt)

Shared Reading

Morning Message

MATERIALS

✓ chart paper or dry erase board
✓ markers or dry erase markers
✓ Wikki Stix® (optional)
✓ reading stick

Turn your morning message into a bug hunt. This activity is a great way to introduce your new theme. Write a message (see sample below) on chart paper or a dry erase board each morning. As you write, invite children to help you sound out words, spell words, and decide what to write. Create a "secret code," and write a "secret message" for children to decode each day. Write the alphabet, and write a number above each letter (e.g., A–1, Z–26), or put numbers below your posted alphabet. Beneath the morning message, draw a blank and a number for each letter of the secret message (butterfly).

Dear Bug Buddies in Room ___,
Today is Friday, April ___, 200___.
We will go on a bug hunt today.
Can you read my code to see what bug we will find?

___ ___ ___ ___ ___ ___ ___ ___
2   21 20 20 5   18 6   12 25

1	2	3	4	5	6	7
A	B	C	D	E	F	G
8	9	10	11	12	13	14
H	I	J	K	L	M	N
15	16	17	18	19	20	21
O	P	Q	R	S	T	U
22	23	24	25	26		
V	W	X	Y	Z		

Invite children to write in the room number and date with a marker or dry erase marker. Have them circle letters, words, or punctuation they know with a marker, a dry erase marker, or Wikki Stix. Depending on the level of the children, leave complete words or word chunks deleted for them to fill in. Have volunteers write the missing letters in the coded message. Have children read aloud the completed message. Choose a child to be the "bug buddy of the day," and invite him or her to use a reading stick (see page 15) to track and reread the morning message.

Pocket Chart Stories

M A T E R I A L S

✓ mini-book reproducibles
(pages 16–19 and 20–23)
✓ sentence strips
✓ pocket chart
✓ sticky notes

Choose a mini-book, and write each sentence on a separate sentence strip. Highlight key words by writing them in a different color to help children easily recognize them. Place the sentence strips in a pocket chart. Make copies of the mini-book pictures, color them, and place each picture next to the matching sentence. For *A Spider on Me!*, discuss why a spider is not a bug. (It is an arachnid because it has eight legs while bugs have six legs.) Have the class read aloud the story while you track and stress high-frequency words. Invite the class to revisit the story. Select a word, letter, or part of a word, and cover it with a sticky note. Invite children to use reading strategies to identify the selected word. Remind them to look at the beginning sound and to decide if their answer makes sense in the sentence.

Sentence Puzzle

M A T E R I A L S

✓ sentence strips
✓ pocket chart

Choose a sentence strip from the pocket chart story (see above), and cut it apart to create word cards. Pass out the cards, and have children read aloud their word. Invite children with word cards to stand up and arrange their words so they form a sentence. Have them put the cards back in the pocket chart in the correct order.

Guided Reading

Assembling the Mini-Books and Reading Sticks

Ⓜ Ⓐ Ⓣ Ⓔ Ⓡ Ⓘ Ⓐ Ⓛ Ⓢ

✓ mini-book reproducibles (pages 16–19 and 20–23)
✓ construction paper
✓ plastic spider rings tied on to curling ribbon
✓ craft sticks
✓ stickers or small objects
✓ envelopes

Make single-sided copies of the reproducibles for each mini-book. Cut each page in half, and staple the pages inside a construction paper cover. For *Giant Bugs, Little Bugs,* invite children to trace their hand on construction paper, cut out their tracing, and glue it over the mosquito on the cover as if they were swatting it. For *A Spider on Me!,* hole-punch the cover, and tie a piece of curling ribbon with a plastic spider ring through the hole. (You can cut out each body shape to make it a shape book.)

Reading sticks help children with one-to-one correspondence and left-to-right directionality and are fun to use. To make a reading stick, glue to the end of a craft stick a sticker or small object that relates to the theme of the mini-book. For example, use a bug sticker for *Giant Bugs, Little Bugs* and a small plastic spider for *A Spider on Me!* Seal envelopes, and cut them in half. Glue each envelope to the front inside cover of a mini-book to make a "pocket." Place a reading stick in the pocket.

Sight Word Practice

Ⓜ Ⓐ Ⓣ Ⓔ Ⓡ Ⓘ Ⓐ Ⓛ Ⓢ

✓ assembled mini-books (see above)
✓ assembled reading sticks (see above)
✓ art supplies

After children review the mini-book text in a shared reading lesson (see page 14), have them write the missing sight words in the blanks to complete their mini-book. In *Giant Bugs, Little Bugs,* the sight word is *here.* In *A Spider on Me!,* the sight words are *is* and *on.* Have children write the name of another person in the last blank on page 8. Then, invite children to decorate their covers and color the illustrations in their books. Have children use reading sticks to help them track words as they read the stories in guided reading groups. As children read *A Spider on Me!,* have them place their spider ring on the correct body part on each page.

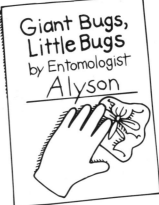

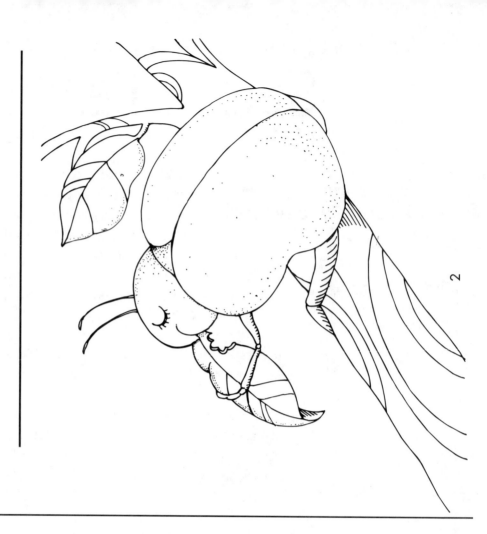

2

Dedicated to

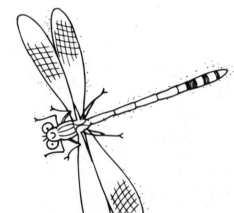

Giant Bugs, Little Bugs

by
Entomologist

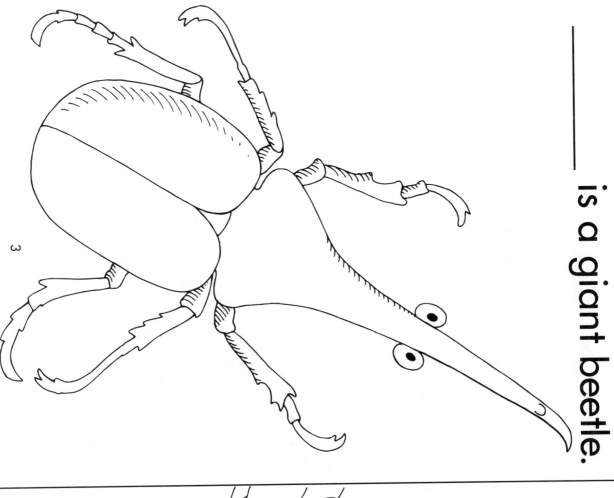

_____ is a giant beetle.

3

_____ is a little caterpillar.

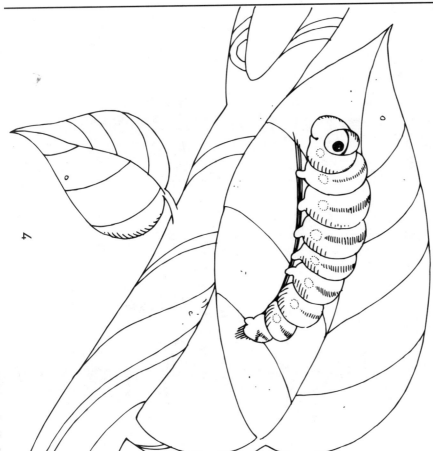

4

_____ is a little

grasshopper.

6

_____ is a giant army

ant.

5

_____ is a giant butterfly.

7

_____ is a little mosquito.

Swat!

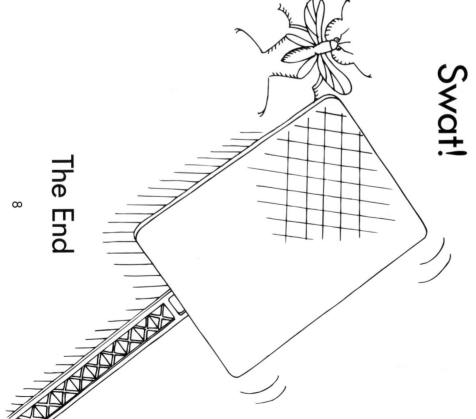

The End

8

A spider _____ my shoe.

2

A Spider on Me!

by

_____

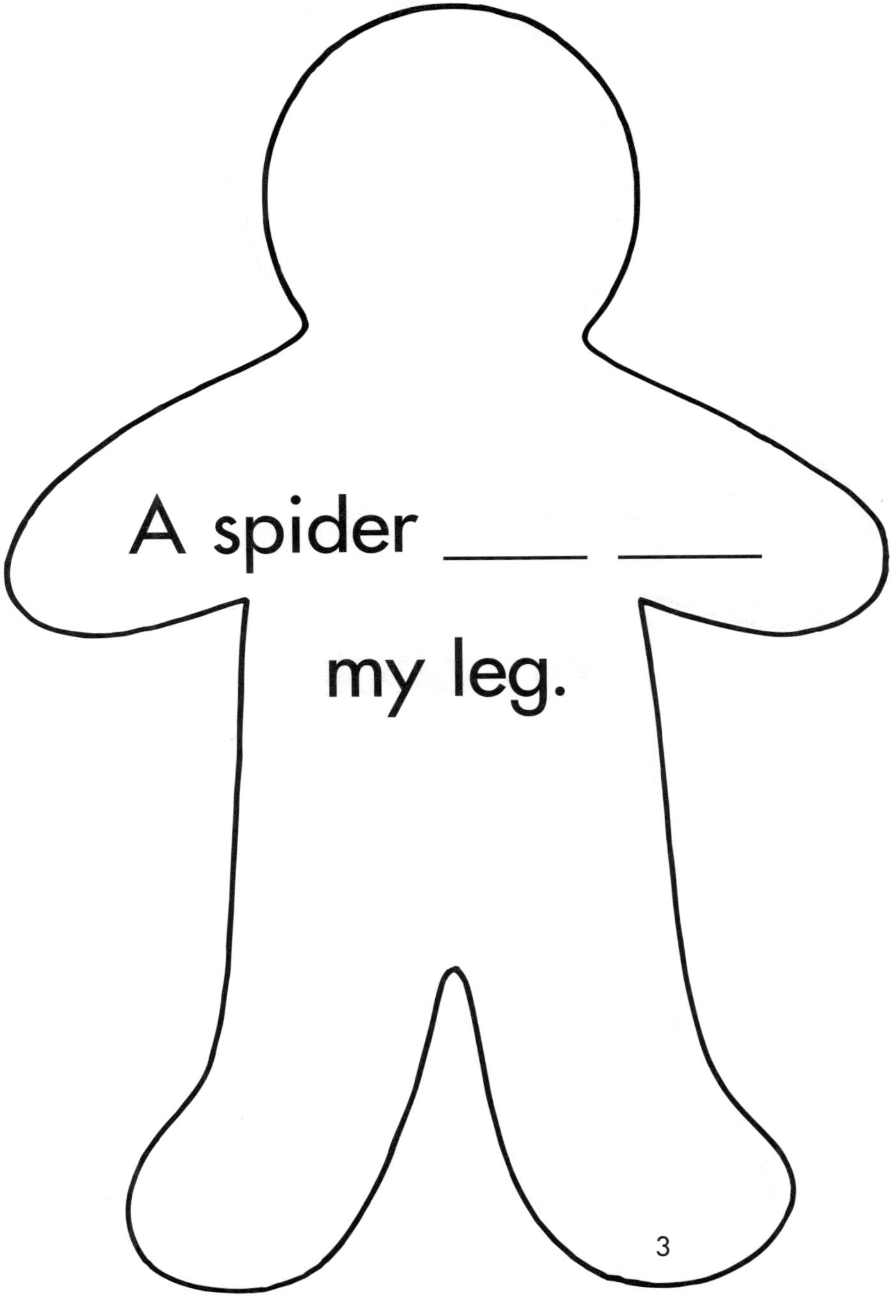

A spider

my leg.

3

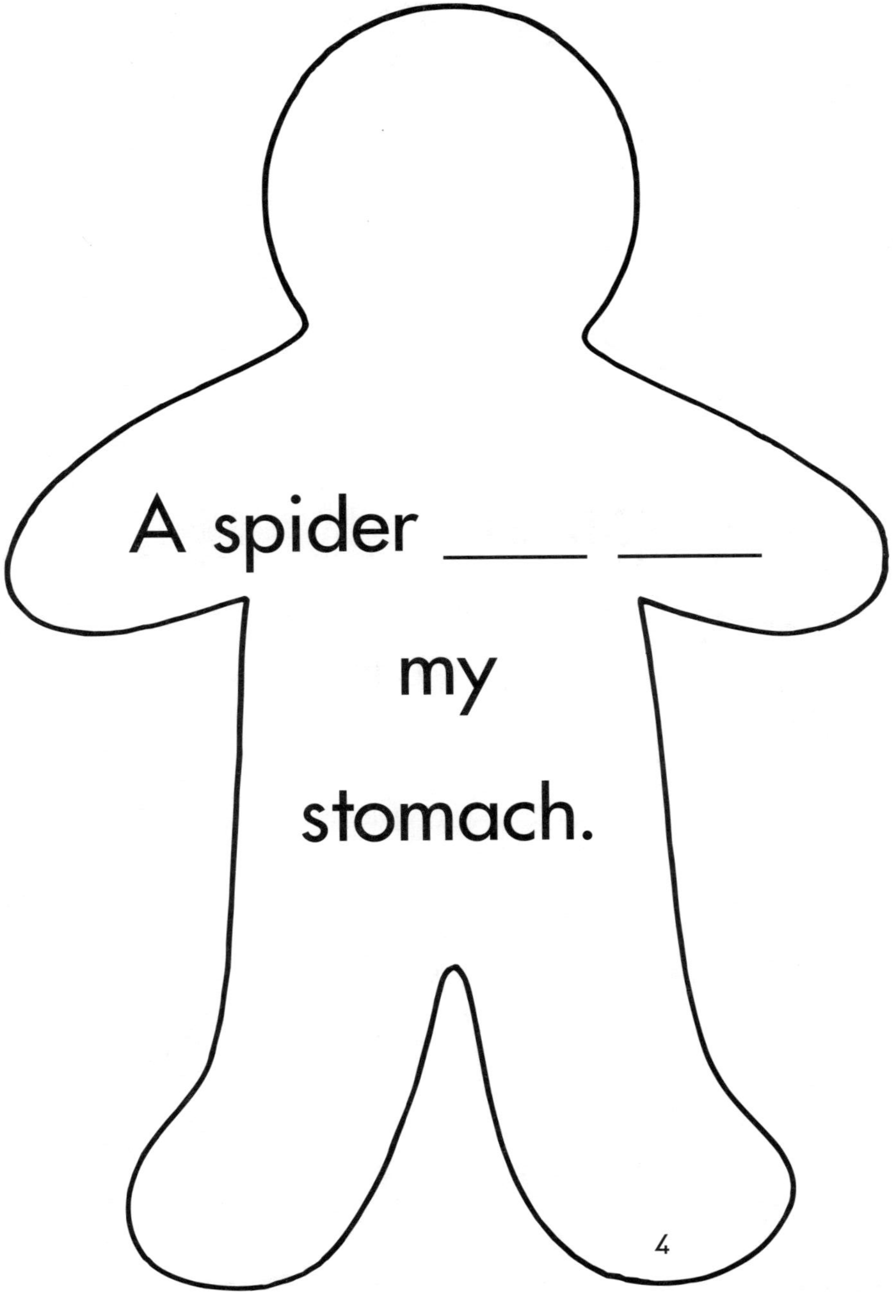

A spider

my stomach.

4

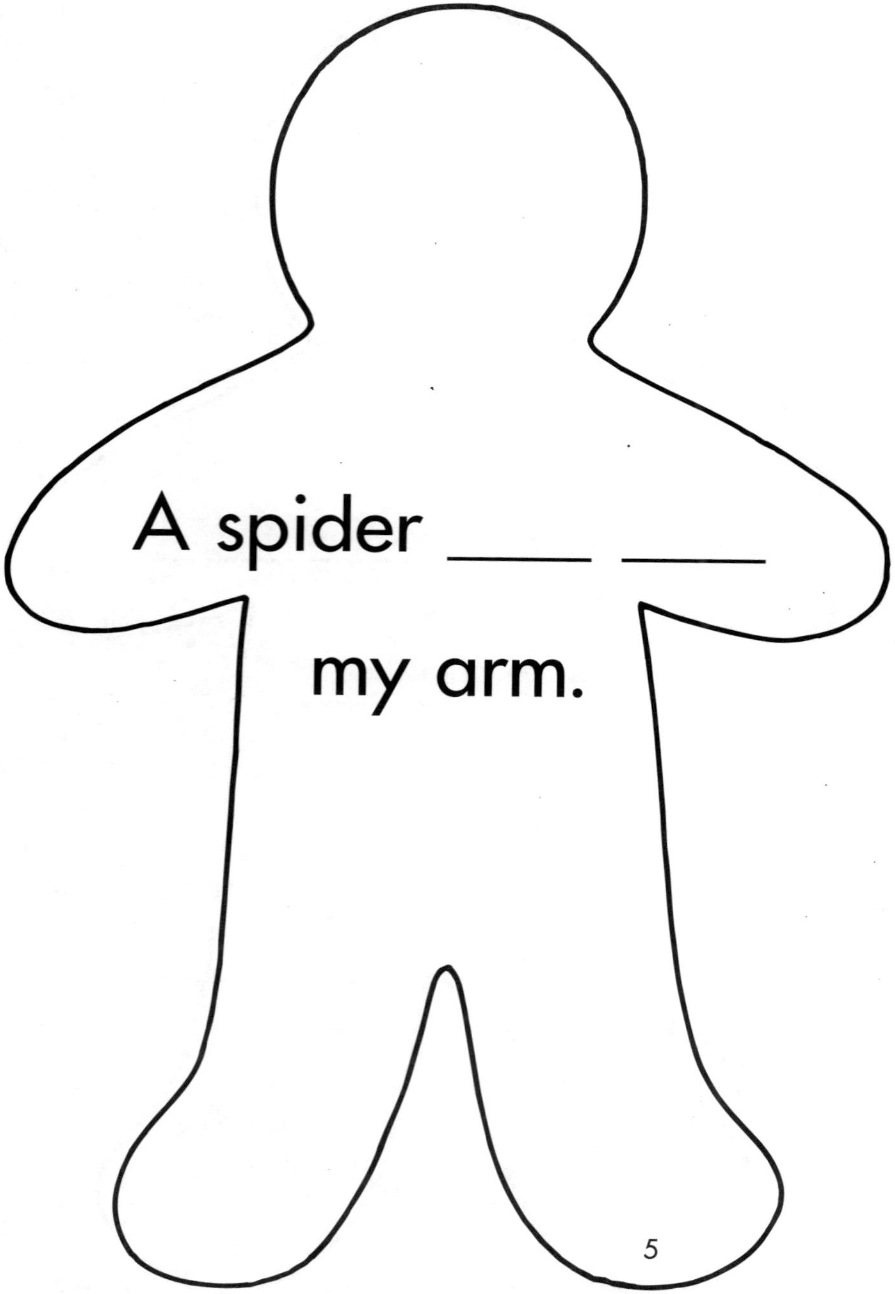

A spider ___ my neck.

6

A spider ___ my arm.

5

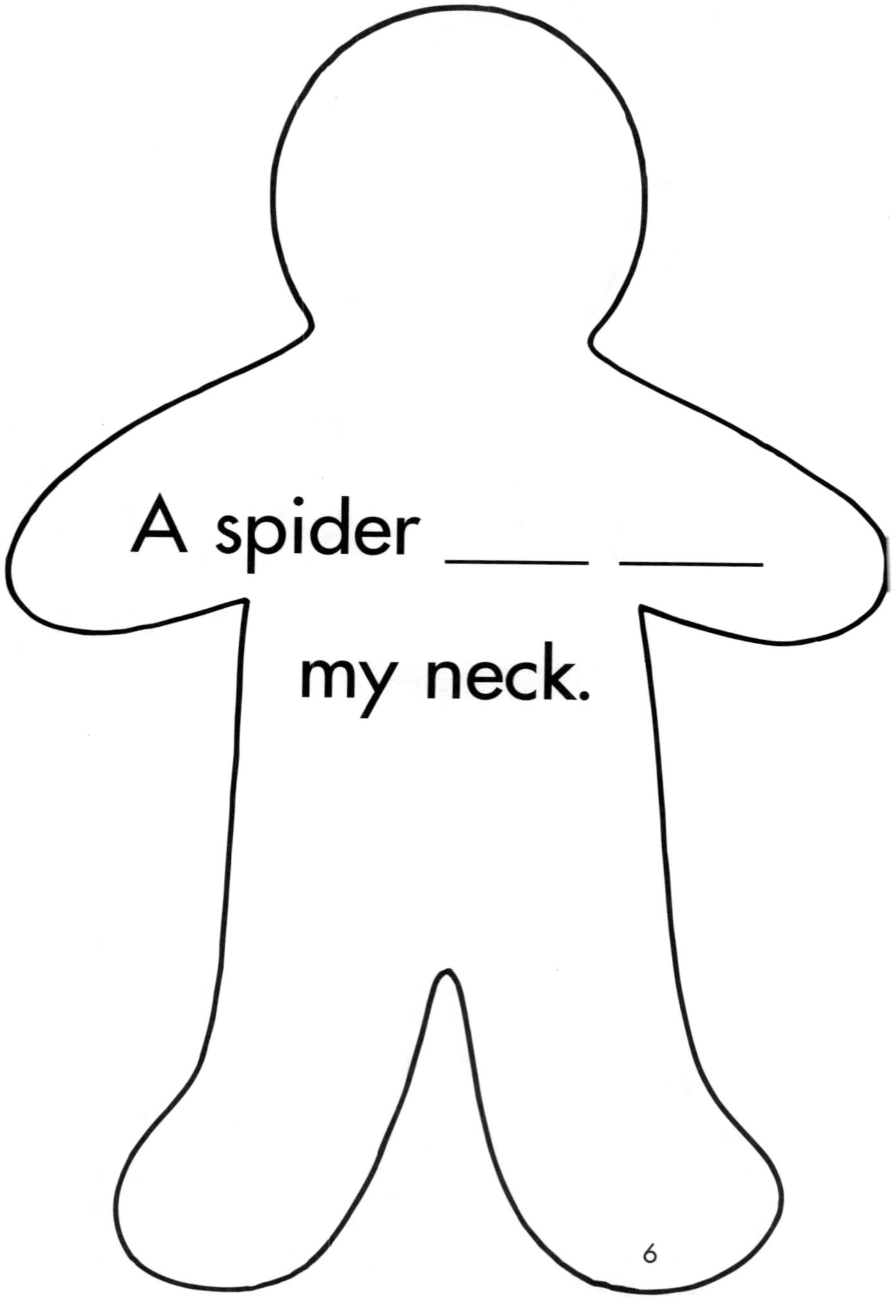

A spider _____
my head.

7

A spider _____
_____!

The End

8

Independent Reading

Swat That Bug at Home!

Copy the Swat That Bug Family Letter, and attach it to a canvas tote bag that each child will take turns bringing home. Use puffy paints to write *Swat That Bug!* on the bag, and hot-glue plastic bugs on it. Copy the Bug Props reproducibles, cut apart the bugs, and mount them on colored construction paper squares. Use a marker to write high-frequency words (e.g., like, is, have) on each square, and laminate the squares. Place books about bugs, the "bug squares," and a flyswatter in the canvas bag. Send home the bag with a different child each night. Ask children to read the books about bugs with their family and practice reading the high-frequency words.

MATERIALS

✓ nonfiction and fiction books about bugs
✓ Swat That Bug Family Letter (page 25)
✓ Bug Props reproducibles (pages 28–29)
✓ canvas tote bag
✓ puffy paints
✓ hot-glue gun
✓ plastic bugs
✓ construction paper squares
✓ flyswatter

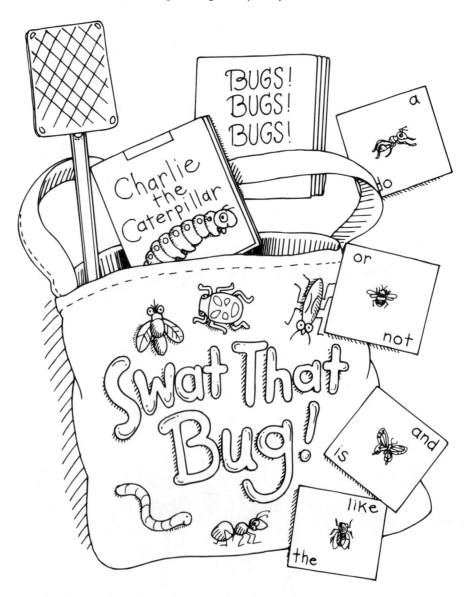

Swat That Bug Family Letter

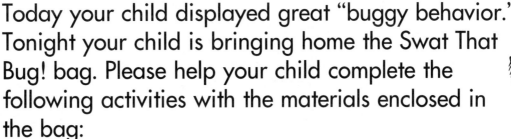

Dear Family,

Today your child displayed great "buggy behavior." Tonight your child is bringing home the Swat That Bug! bag. Please help your child complete the following activities with the materials enclosed in the bag:

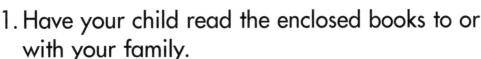

1. Have your child read the enclosed books to or with your family.

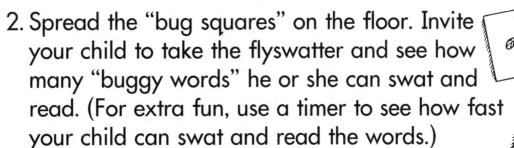

2. Spread the "bug squares" on the floor. Invite your child to take the flyswatter and see how many "buggy words" he or she can swat and read. (For extra fun, use a timer to see how fast your child can swat and read the words.)

3. Have your child practice writing the words on a piece of paper. How many words can he or she spell?

4. Place all of the items back in the bag and return it to school tomorrow for another Bug Friend to enjoy!

Thank you for your help with this fun home activity.

Sincerely,

A Butterfly Birthday Party

MATERIALS

✓ *Miss Spider's Tea Party* by David Kirk
✓ A Butterfly Birthday Party reproducible (page 27)
✓ Bug Props reproducibles (pages 28–29)
✓ sentence strips
✓ fresh or silk flowers
✓ birthday party invitations
✓ color transparency of a garden
✓ overhead projector
✓ art supplies

Culminate your bug unit by inviting your class to perform a dramatic play that highlights what they learned. Read aloud *Miss Spider's Tea Party.* (The dramatic play is an innovation of this story.) Then, read aloud the play on the A Butterfly Birthday Party reproducible to introduce children to the characters and their lines. Assign every child a part. (Have one child be the butterfly and numerous children be grasshoppers, ants, ladybugs, bees, and flies.) Make enlarged copies of the Bug Props reproducibles, and give each child the corresponding cutout to color. Invite children to glue their bug to a sentence strip to make a headband. Project the transparency onto a blank wall as the backdrop for the dramatic play. Have children practice their lines until they comfortably know them and are ready to perform in front of an audience of peers or parents. For extra fun, place a tablecloth on the floor with party plates, napkins, cups, and a pretend birthday cake on it. (This dramatic play can be sung to the tune of "Clementine.")

A Butterfly Birthday Party

 Butterfly: (holding invitations) It's my birthday! It's my birthday! It's a party just for me! I'll invite my buggy buddies, and we'll have a cup of tea! Hi buggy buddies! (hand out invitations)

 Grasshoppers: (holding flowers) We're the grasshoppers, we're the grasshoppers on the way to the party! Let's bring a flower for the butterfly and have a cup of tea! (hand butterfly the flowers)

 Ants: (holding flowers) We're the ants, we're the ants on the way to the party! Let's bring a flower for the butterfly and have a cup of tea! (hand butterfly the flowers)

 Ladybugs: (holding flowers) We're the ladybugs, we're the ladybugs on the way to the party! Let's bring a flower for the butterfly and have a cup of tea! (hand butterfly the flowers)

 Bees: (holding flowers) We're the bees, we're the bees on the way to the party! Let's bring a flower for the butterfly and have a cup of tea! (hand butterfly the flowers)

 Flies: (holding flowers) We're the flies, we're the flies on the way to the party! Let's bring a flower for the butterfly and have a cup of tea! (hand butterfly the flowers)

 Butterfly: It's my birthday! It's my birthday! I had so much fun! I love all the flowers, and I'll nibble every one!

 Grasshoppers, Ants, Ladybugs, Bees, Flies: Happy birthday, Butterfly!

Bug Props

Going Buggy! © 2003 Creative Teaching Press

Bug Props

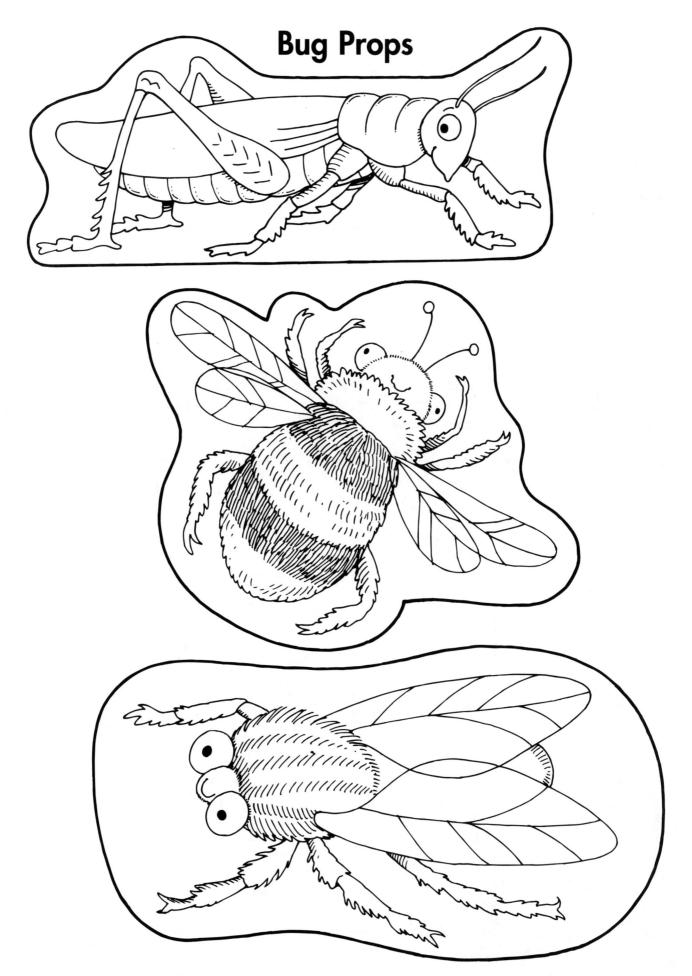

Shared Writing

A "Webby" Word Wall

MATERIALS

✓ black butcher paper
✓ silver glitter
✓ construction paper
✓ spider stuffed animal
✓ dowel
✓ curling ribbon
✓ art supplies

Create a bug word wall with your class. Paint a large white spiderweb on black butcher paper, and sprinkle silver glitter on the paint while it is still wet. (Optional: For a fun display, hot-glue plastic bugs on the web.) Have children help you spell and sound out names of bugs and key words such as *wings*, *antennae*, and *spider*. Write each word in bold dark colors on a piece of construction paper, and cut it out in its lettered shape. (You can write vowels in a different color to help children identify them.) Glue these words (in alphabetical order or randomly) to your spiderweb, and display it on a classroom wall for whole-class reference. Reread the words for a daily shared reading experience using a reading stick. Cut a small hole in a spider stuffed animal, glue it to a dowel, and attach black and red curling ribbon to the dowel to make a fun reading stick. Remind children to refer to these words for independent, interactive, and shared writing activities.

Bug Hunting

M A T E R I A L S

✓ large sheets of lined paper
✓ construction paper
✓ plastic bugs or bug stickers
✓ art supplies

Staple a sheet of lined paper for each child between two sheets of construction paper to make a class Big Book. Make a construction paper "box" by cutting out a rectangle and folding over the top of it to make a "lid." Glue plastic bugs or bug stickers under the lid, and glue the box on the cover. Write on the cover the title *Bug Hunting*. Sing the following song to the tune of "A-Hunting We Will Go" with the class.

A-Bug-Hunting We Will Go!

A-bug-hunting we will go.
A-bug-hunting we will go.
We will catch a bug
And put it in a box
And then we'll let it go!

Make a construction paper box for each child. Each day, choose a different child to be the "bug buddy of the day," and have the class sing the song. Ask each bug buddy of the day the same questions to complete the following sentence frame: *(Child's name) will catch a (bug name) and put it in a box and then he'll/she'll let it go!* Then, sing the song a second time using the child's responses in the third through fifth lines (e.g., *Artie will catch a ladybug and put*

it in a box and then he'll let it go!). Write children's responses on separate pages in the Big Book. Ask children to help you sound out words to spell them. Give children a construction paper box, and invite them to draw their bug or put a plastic bug or sticker inside their box. Glue children's boxes on the page with their responses on it. Each day, begin the activity by rereading the previous days' pages for shared reading.

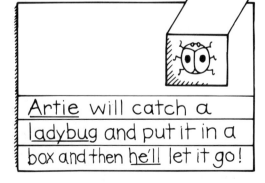

Interactive Writing

Fantastic Fly Facts

MATERIALS

✓ *Bugs and Slugs* by Judy Tatchell
✓ black butcher paper
✓ waxed paper
✓ construction paper strips
✓ flyswatter

Draw a large fly on black butcher paper, and attach waxed paper wings. Read aloud the pages in *Bugs and Slugs* that focus on flies, and discuss fly facts with the class. Use interactive writing to have children take turns writing facts about flies on construction paper strips. Invite children to reread the sentences for shared reading and use a flyswatter as a reading stick. Glue the paper strips to the fly, and hang it on a wall or chart rack. To extend the activity, read aloud books about other bugs, have children write facts about them, and display them on bug-shaped pieces of butcher paper.

Flies taste with their feet.

Flies have compound eyes.

Yuck! No!

MATERIALS

✓ *The Roly Poly Spider*
  by Jill Sardegna
✓ construction paper
✓ paper plates
✓ napkins
✓ art supplies

Read aloud *The Roly Poly Spider*. Divide the class into groups of two or three children. Have each group choose a bug to pretend to eat and cut out several of that bug from construction paper. Tell groups to glue their bugs onto a paper plate. (Have one group make a plate of "cookies.") Invite groups to glue their plate to a large sheet of construction paper and glue a napkin next to the plate. Collect the papers, and use interactive writing to have children write below each plate sentences that follow the sentence frames *Do you eat (name of bug)? Yuck! No!* On the paper with the plate of cookies, have children write *Do you eat cookies? Yum! Yes!* Invite groups to stand in front of the class and share their picture and sentences. Have the group with the plate of cookies read aloud their page last. Bind all the pages into a class book for rereading.

Guided Writing

I'm as Quick as a . . .

MATERIALS

✓ I'm as Quick as a Cricket by Audrey Wood
✓ chart paper
✓ white construction paper
✓ art supplies

Read aloud *I'm as Quick as a Cricket*. Discuss the characteristic of each animal in the book that makes it similar to human beings (e.g., slow as a snail). At the top of a piece of chart paper, write *I'm as Quick as a . . . .* Below the title, write the sentence frame "*I am as quick as a _____,*" said _____. Complete the sentence frame (e.g., "*I am as quick as a rabbit,*" said Ms. Lee), and write it on the chart paper. Invite children to independently complete the sentence frame and write their sentence on the chart paper below your sentence. Invite them to write during circle time, center time, or independent writing time. Tell children to follow the frame you wrote as they write their own answer. Remind children to use "temporary spelling" when they write their sentence.

After all the sentences are written (this may take a few days), type all the sentences and give each child his or her sentence. Tell children to read their sentence and then cut it apart so each word is separate. Have children mix up the words and then put them back in order to create their sentence. Invite children to glue their word cards to the bottom of a piece of white construction paper. Then, invite children to illustrate their sentence. Bind children's pages together to create a class book. Encourage children to independently read the book.

A Baggy Full of Bugs

✓ *Bugs! Bugs! Bugs!* by Bob Barner
✓ Bug Cards (page 11)
✓ Colorful Bugs reproducible (page 36)
✓ sandwich-size resealable plastic bags (7 for each child)
✓ colored masking tape
✓ art supplies

Staple together on the bottom seam seven plastic bags for each child. Use colored tape to seal together the bags (over the staples to keep them from poking children). Read aloud *Bugs! Bugs! Bugs!*, and discuss the characteristics and colors of different bugs. Give each child a copy of the Bug Cards and the Colorful Bugs reproducible. Have children cut apart the bugs and the sentence strips. Tell them to set aside the stink bug from the Colorful Bugs reproducible. Invite children to choose six bugs, color each bug a different color (one must be pink), and color the stink bug black. Have them complete a sentence strip for each bug by writing <u>A</u> bug <u>can</u> be (<u>color</u>). Then, have children put each colored bug and each matching sentence in a separate bag. Tell them to put the pink bug and its matching sentence in the second to last bag and the stink bug and its matching sentence (i.e., *A bug can really stink!*) in the last bag.

ladybug

<u>A</u> bug <u>can</u> be <u>red</u>.

Colorful Bugs

_____ bug _____ be _____.

_____ bug _____ be _____.

_____ bug _____ be _____.

_____ bug _____ be _____.

_____ bug _____ be _____.

_____ bug _____ be _____.

A bug can really stink!

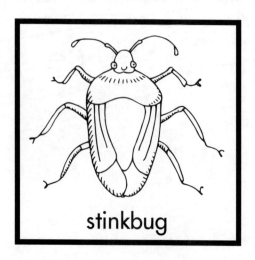

stinkbug

Independent Writing

Rhyming Bees

MATERIALS

✓ chart paper
✓ white sticky labels
✓ construction paper
✓ newspaper
✓ waxed paper
✓ art supplies

Ask children to brainstorm words that rhyme with *bee*. Write their responses on chart paper. Have each child choose a different word from the list and write it on a white sticky label. Give each child a large piece of white construction paper, and ask children to paint yellow and black stripes on it. Let the paint dry. Have children use an oval pattern to cut out two bee bodies. Glue together the bodies, leaving an opening, and have children stuff their bee with newspaper. Have children cut out two small waxed paper circles and attach them to the top of their bee to create "wings." Invite children to cut construction paper to make eyes and a stinger and attach them to their bee. Ask children to place their sticky label on one side of their bee. Encourage children to write other words that rhyme with *bee* on additional labels and put them on their bee. For a fun display, make a "beehive" to hang near children's work. Paint 36 toilet paper rolls brown. When the paint is dry, glue eight toilet paper rolls together to form the bottom row. Then, glue seven on top to make the next row, six on top of that, and so forth until you glue one toilet paper roll on top. Add yellow paint to the opening of one side of each roll to look like honey. Display children's writing and bees with the beehive.

Fantastic Fireflies

M A T E R I A L S

✓ *The Very Lonely Firefly* by Eric Carle
✓ Jar and Fireflies reproducible (page 39)
✓ construction paper
✓ art supplies

Copy a class set of the Jar and Fireflies reproducible on white construction paper. Read aloud *The Very Lonely Firefly*. Decide what skill you would like children to practice (e.g., writing ABC's, numbers to 30, sight word practice). Have children use independent writing to complete the sentence frame at the bottom of the reproducible. For example, children might write *TJ* can *write the alphabet* or *Chelsy* can *write numbers*. Then, invite children to demonstrate their skill by filling in the lines at the top of their paper. For example, children might write the letters of the alphabet or the numbers from 1 to 30. Invite children to cut out their jar, trace it on black construction paper, and cut out the black jar to make a cover. Then, have children cut out the fireflies from their reproducible, color them yellow, and use glitter glue to make their tails "light up." You can also have children add a thumbprint on the center of each firefly with neon paint. Staple each child's black jar on top of the white jar, and have children glue their fireflies on the cover. For a fun display, hang children's work on a bulletin board with twinkling holiday lights as a border. Encourage children to read each other's work.

Jar and Fireflies

_____ can_____

_____ .

Math

Caterpillar Inches

MATERIALS

✓ *Inch by Inch* by Leo Lionni
✓ pipe cleaners
✓ rulers
✓ linking cubes
✓ construction paper
✓ long green butcher paper strips
✓ art supplies

Cut a class set of pipe cleaners into 6" (15 cm) strips. Read aloud *Inch by Inch* to introduce children to measurement. Have children practice measuring items in the classroom with standard (e.g., rulers), and nonstandard (e.g., linking cubes) measuring tools.

Give each child a pipe cleaner and two different colored sheets of construction paper. Have children cut out small construction paper circles (about 2 inches or 5 cm round). Hole-punch the center of children's circles. Ask children to slide their circles on the pipe cleaner in a pattern to form a "caterpillar body." Have them cut out a head and glue it around one end of their pipe cleaner. Put a piece of masking tape around the other end of each pipe cleaner to prevent children's circles from sliding off. Then, invite children to paint a large construction paper flower (not the stem) or make handprint "petals" around the center of a large circle to make a flower. Give each child a long strip of green paper to make a "stem" for their flower. Have children tape the stem to the back of their flower and cut it to whatever length they choose.

Invite children to measure the length of their flower with their caterpillar. Have them place their caterpillar at the bottom of the stem and measure how many caterpillars tall the flower is. (You may want children to work in pairs so one child can use his or her finger as a spacer for the caterpillar.) Have children write and complete the sentence frame *My flower is ___ caterpillars tall.* Display children's flowers and writing on a bulletin board. Write at the top of the bulletin board *Inch by inch. Look how we can pattern. We know how to measure.*

My flower is **10** caterpillars tall.

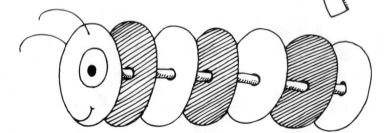

The Buggy Backpack

MATERIALS

- ✓ 1 fiction and 1 nonfiction book about bugs
- ✓ Bug Backpack Family Letter (page 42)
- ✓ construction paper
- ✓ plastic bugs
- ✓ large plastic jar with a lid
- ✓ hot-glue gun
- ✓ backpack
- ✓ plastic magnifying glass

Copy the Bug Backpack Family Letter on construction paper. Put plastic bugs into a large jar with a lid, and hot-glue plastic bugs on a backpack. Put the letter, bug books, jar, and a magnifying glass in the backpack. Send home the backpack with a different child each night. Ask children to read the bug books to or with their family and complete several math activities with the jar of bugs.

Ladybug Clock

MATERIALS

- ✓ *The Grouchy Ladybug* by Eric Carle
- ✓ Ladybug Body reproducible (page 43)
- ✓ Ladybug Clock reproducible (page 44)
- ✓ tagboard
- ✓ construction paper
- ✓ wiggly eyes
- ✓ small paper plates
- ✓ brass fasteners
- ✓ art supplies

Make several copies of the Ladybug Body reproducible on tagboard, and cut them out to make patterns for children to trace. Read aloud *The Grouchy Ladybug,* and discuss telling time to the hour with the class. Invite children to make a "ladybug clock." Have each child trace a ladybug body pattern on black construction paper and cut it out. Invite children to add wiggly eyes and six construction paper legs to their ladybug. Tell them to paint a paper plate red and then cut it in half to create "wings." Have them add black spots to the wings and staple the wings to their bug body. Give each child a Ladybug Clock reproducible, and have children cut out their clock. Use brass fasteners to attach each child's clock hands to his or her clock. Then, glue the outer edge of the clocks to the underside of children's bug bodies. (Make sure to only glue the outer edge so the clock hands will move.) Reread the book, and have children manipulate the hands on their clock to match the times in the story. To extend the activity, have children practice telling time to the half hour or in 15-minute increments.

Bug Backpack Family Letter

Dear Family,

Your little entomologist is bringing home the Buggy Backpack to share with you! Our class has been learning about bugs. Tonight your child is going to take a closer look at the shapes and sizes of bugs and use them in math activities. Read the enclosed stories with your child and discuss why one of the books is factual and the other is fictional. Then, help your child complete the following activities:

1. Invite your child to sort the bugs. How many different ways can he or she sort them? (color, size, shape, spots)

2. Have your child make patterns with the bugs. What is the most complex pattern he or she can make?

3. Tell your child to count how many bugs are in the jar. Can he or she skip count by 2s? 5s? 10s?

Have a "Buggy Time"!

Please be sure to put all the items back in the Buggy Backpack so that another little entomologist can take this bag home tomorrow.

Sincerely,

Ladybug Body

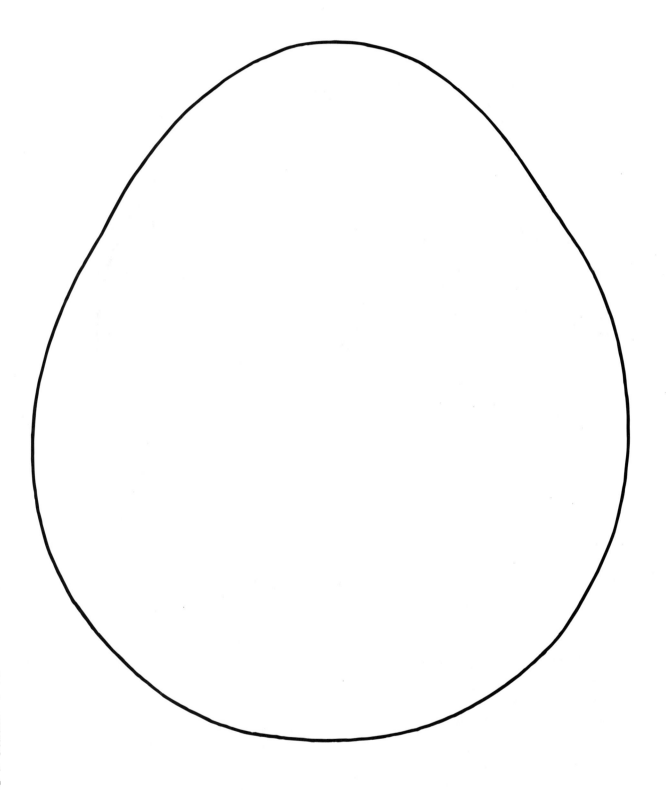

Ladybug Clock

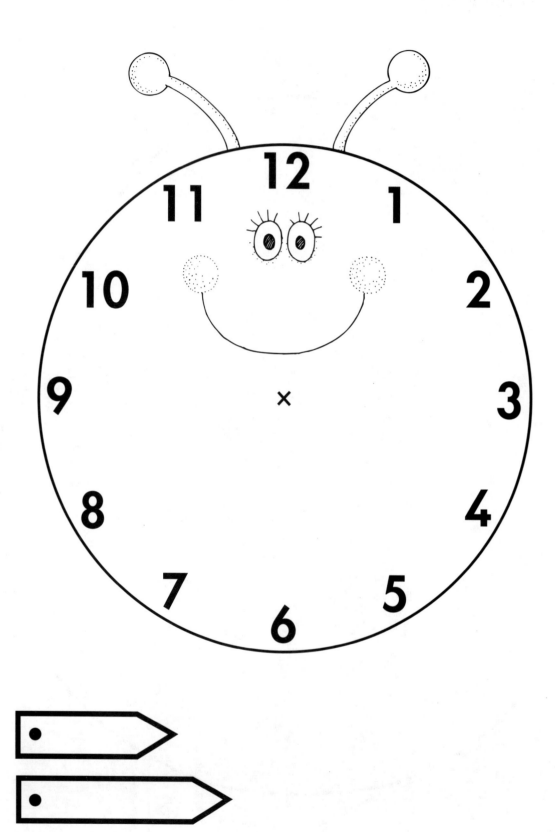

How Many Bugs?

Read aloud *How Many Bugs in a Box?* Give each child a paper bag, and help children make a paper "box." (See the steps below.) Choose a target number that children will use to write addition problems. Give each child a copy of the Bug Cards, and have children color the same number of bugs as the target number, cut them apart, and put them in their box. Give each child construction paper strips (one more than the chosen number). Have children use their bugs to make number combinations and write addition equations on the paper strips. For example, if you chose the number 7, give children eight construction paper strips, and children will write the equations $0 + 7 = 7$, $1 + 6 = 7$, $2 + 5 = 7$, and so forth. Staple together each child's strips to make "number books." Have children keep their book and bugs in their box. Invite children to use these materials for ongoing counting and addition practice.

MATERIALS

✓ *How Many Bugs in a Box?* by David Carter
✓ Bug Cards (page 11)
✓ lunch-size brown paper bags
✓ pipe cleaners
✓ white construction paper strips
✓ bug stickers
✓ art supplies

How to Make a Paper Box

Step 1: Cut a bag on the folds. Start cutting at the top and stop where the natural crease is on the bottom (about 2 inches or 5 cm up from the bottom). Make four cuts.

Step 2: Fold three sides in, leaving the back flap out. (The box should be taking shape.)

Step 3: Fold the back flap over once and attach a small pipe cleaner handle.

Step 4: Decorate your box with bug stickers.

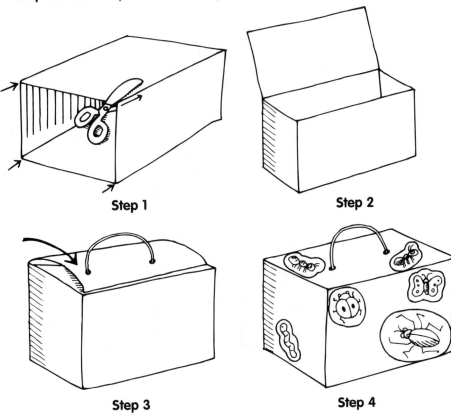

Step 1

Step 2

Step 3

Step 4

Buzzing Bugs Glyph

✓ Bug Glyph Key reproducible (page 47)
✓ cardboard apple packing material (from the produce department)
✓ wiggly eyes
✓ construction paper
✓ cellophane
✓ art supplies

Cut apple packing material into two connected pieces (see drawing below) so each child has one. Copy the Bug Glyph Key reproducible, and display it. Have children refer to the key as they make a bug. Have all children paint the head of their bug black and add wiggly eyes when the paint is dry. Then, have them paint the body their favorite color. Have them add spots or stripes to represent their age. Tell children to add black or brown construction paper legs to show whether they do or don't like bugs. Ask them to add cellophane wings if they have flown on an airplane. Display children's bugs and the glyph key on a bulletin board. Have children analyze the data on each bug by referring to the glyph key. For example, a child might say *Scott's favorite color is blue because his bug's body is blue. He likes bugs because he attached black legs. He is 6 years old because there are 6 spots on his bug. His bug doesn't have wings so he has never flown on an airplane.*

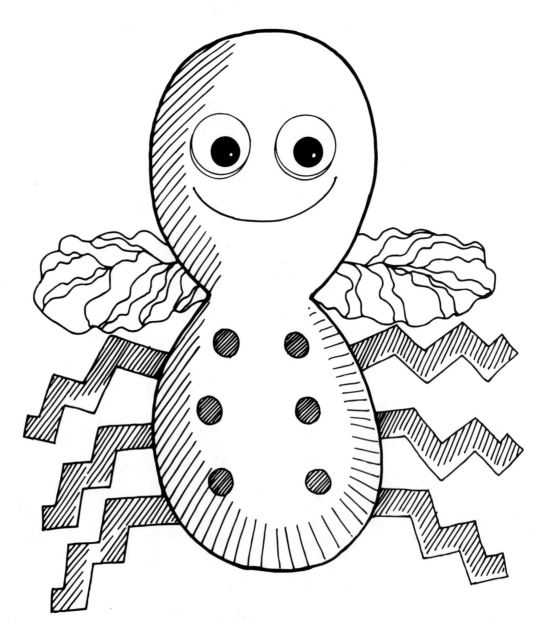

Bug Glyph Key

1 <u>What is your favorite color?</u>
Paint the bug's body your favorite color.

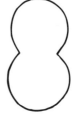

2 <u>How old are you?</u>
Paint the same number of spots or stripes as your age.

3 <u>Do you like bugs?</u>
Add black legs if you like bugs.

Add brown legs if you do not like bugs.

4 <u>Have you flown on an airplane?</u>
Add wings if you have flown on an airplane.

Do not add wings if you have not flown on an airplane.

Caterpillar Film Canisters

MATERIALS

✓ *The Very Hungry Caterpillar* by Eric Carle
✓ chart paper
✓ register tape
✓ construction paper
✓ empty film canisters (1 for each child)
✓ white sticky labels

Read aloud *The Very Hungry Caterpillar*, and review the sequence of the story (i.e., caterpillar, the fruits, the cocoon, the butterfly). Record the sequence on chart paper by drawing simple pictures. Then, give each child a long strip of register tape. Have each child cut out construction paper pieces to illustrate the sequence of the story. Tell children to cut out a caterpillar, one apple, two pears, three oranges, and so forth. Have them glue the cutouts in order to the register tape, ending with the chrysalis and butterfly. Ask each child to hole-punch each food and the chrysalis to show where the caterpillar ate through it. Invite children to use their completed register tape to retell the story. Then, have them carefully roll up their tape and place it in a film canister. Tell children to write *The Very Hungry Caterpillar* on a white sticky label and stick it on the front of their film canister.

Colorful Bug Pie Graph

MATERIALS

✓ tagboard
✓ color pictures of bugs
  (1 for each child)
✓ construction paper
✓ magnifying glasses
✓ sentence strips

Draw a bug with a large body on tagboard (see picture below). Draw two large circles (for the pie graph) that will fit on the bug's body. Cut out the circles, and glue one circle on the bug's body. Cut the second circle into equal-sized pie-shaped parts to make enough patterns for each child to trace one. Give each child a color picture of a bug cut from a magazine. Invite children to carefully study the bug in their picture. Tell them to focus their observations on the bug's covering and colors. Have children use magnifying glasses to take a closer look. Discuss how bright colors on a bug may be a warning to birds and lizards that the bug is dangerous. Discuss how some colors are good for camouflage. Ask children to decide what color is the most prominent on their bug, and have them trace and cut out a pie-shaped pattern from that color construction paper. When all of the children have cut out their piece, sort the pieces into color groups, and glue them on the circle on the bug's body to create a pie graph. Invite children to analyze the data on the graph. Ask questions such as *Are there more red, green, black, or yellow bugs?* Write the information on sentence strips. Then, have children figure out what fraction of the bugs are each color, and record the information on sentence strips. For example, if children analyze 20 bugs and 2 of the bugs are green, the fraction would be $2/20$. Display the bug pie graph and sentence strips on a bulletin board with the title *Insect colors so beautiful to me, what color is the most we'll see?*

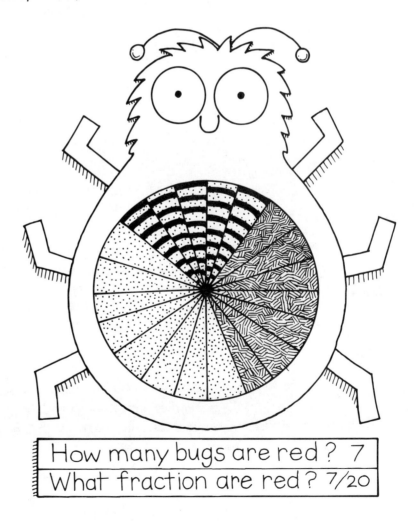

How many bugs are red? 7
What fraction are red? 7/20

Science

Bug Observation Box

✓ Bug Box Observation Sheet (page 51)
✓ empty oatmeal canisters (1 for each child)
✓ sheer white netting or tulle
✓ corks (1 for each child)

Invite children to go on a bug hunt! Assemble a "bug box" for each child by cutting a 4" (10 cm) "window" in the side of an oatmeal canister, and then have children tape a piece of netting or tulle over it to cover the hole. (Children will observe their bug through this hole.) Cut a little hole in one end of each box, and put a cork in it. (This hole is for the bug to go through.) Go on a bug hunt with your class, and have each child collect a bug and put it in a box. Or, have children collect bugs at home. Tell children to add some grass and leaves to their box. Give each child a Bug Box Observation Sheet, and tell children to observe their bug for five days. Have them draw their bug and record their observations on their sheet each day. After five days, have children return the bugs to their outside home.

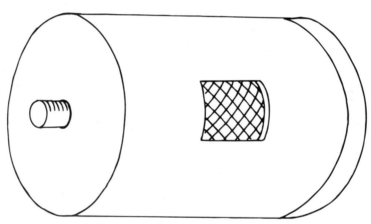

Bug Body Puzzles

✓ "Parts of a Bug" song (page 52)
✓ Bug Puzzles (page 53)
✓ construction paper
✓ chart paper or overhead transparency (optional)
✓ tagboard
✓ resealable plastic bags
✓ art supplies

Copy the song "Parts of a Bug" on construction paper, or write it on chart paper, or use the reproducible to make an overhead transparency to make an enlarged copy. Copy a class set of the Bug Puzzles on tagboard. Discuss bug body parts with the class. Sing the song "Parts of a Bug" to reinforce the different parts of bugs. Give each child a page of puzzle pieces, and invite children to lightly color the bugs and trace the words *antennae, head, thorax,* and *abdomen.* Have children cut out the bug puzzles and then cut apart each bug puzzle on the dotted cut lines. Invite them to practice putting the different bug body parts back together. Tell children to say each part as they do so. Ask children to store their pieces in a plastic bag. (You can type a sentence frame that says _____'s *Buggy Body Bag* and tape it on each bag so children's bags don't get mixed up.) Invite children to bring home their bag and practice putting the puzzles together with their family.

Bug Box Observation Sheet

_____'s Bug Box

My bug is a _____.

Day 1	Day 2
_____	_____
_____	_____
_____	_____
_____	_____

Day 3	Day 4	Day 5
_____	_____	_____
_____	_____	_____
_____	_____	_____
_____	_____	_____

Parts of a Bug

(sing to the tune of "Head, Shoulders, Knees, and Toes")

Antennae,
Head,
Thorax,
Abdomen, abdomen.

Antennae,
Head,
Thorax,
Abdomen, abdomen.

Six legs to help me move all around.
If you see me on the ground,
Don't step on me!

Bug Puzzles

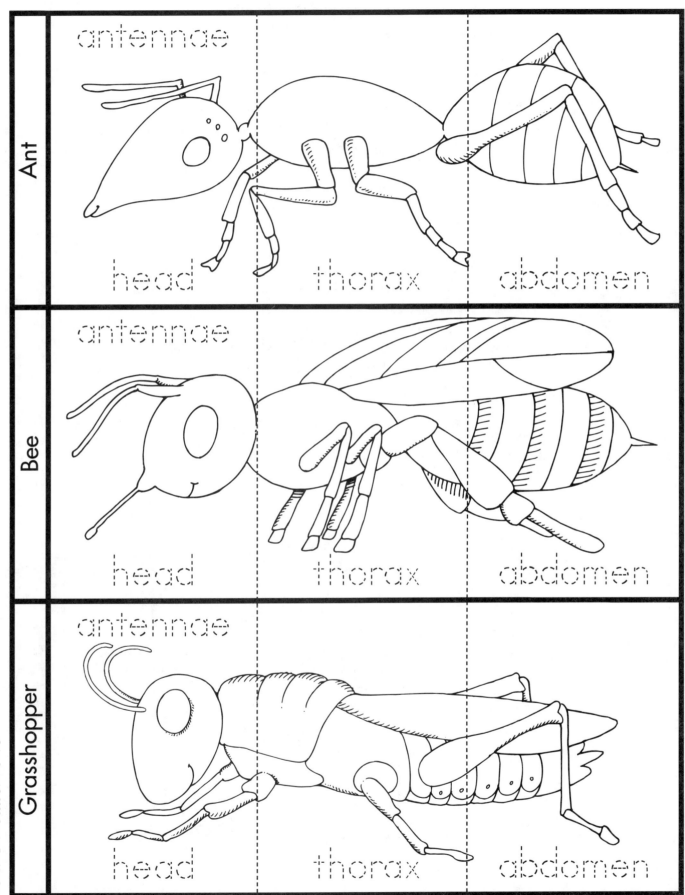

Ant

antennae

head thorax abdomen

Bee

antennae

head thorax abdomen

Grasshopper

antennae

head thorax abdomen

Social Studies

When I Try . . .

Read aloud *The Very Clumsy Click Beetle*, and discuss how the click beetle had difficulty turning over at first, but it really wanted to succeed, so it practiced and practiced to improve, and was finally able to flip over. Tell children that if a task seems too difficult and they really want to succeed, they must practice and practice to improve their skills and they must always try their best! Ask children to give examples of a time they tried their best and learned how to do something. For example, a child might say *When I try, I can tie my shoes* or *When I try, I can dive in the pool.* Record their responses on chart paper. Give each child a sentence frame from the When I Try reproducible, and have children write their example on the reproducible. Then, have children paint an illustration of their sentence on a piece of white construction paper. When the paint is dry, glue each picture to a larger piece of butcher paper, and use colored masking tape to frame the artwork. Glue children's writing below their picture. Display children's work in the classroom for rereading.

When I try, I can ride my bike.

by Armando

When I Try

When I try, I can _____

_____

_____

by _____

When I try, I can _____

_____

_____

by _____

Don't Step on the Ants!

MATERIALS

✓ *Hey, Little Ant* by Phillip and Hannah Hoose
✓ Kindness to All reproducible (page 57)
✓ cardboard apple packing material (from the produce department)
✓ construction paper
✓ wiggly eyes
✓ art supplies

Cut apple packing material into three connected pieces (see drawing below) to make an "ant body" for each child. Read aloud *Hey, Little Ant*. Discuss being kind to others and how people should treat all living things. Give each child a sentence frame from the Kindness to All reproducible. Invite children to complete the frame by writing something they do that shows kindness and consideration for others. For example, children might write *Chelsy* Ant said, "*Say nice things to your friends*." or *Bailey* Ant said, "*I play with everybody*." Give each child an ant body, and have children paint it black or red. Have them add six paper legs, antennae, and two wiggly eyes. Staple each child's sentence frame to his or her ant's back. Staple the ants in a pattern (e.g., black ant, red ant, black ant, red ant) around a doorway or across a windowsill.

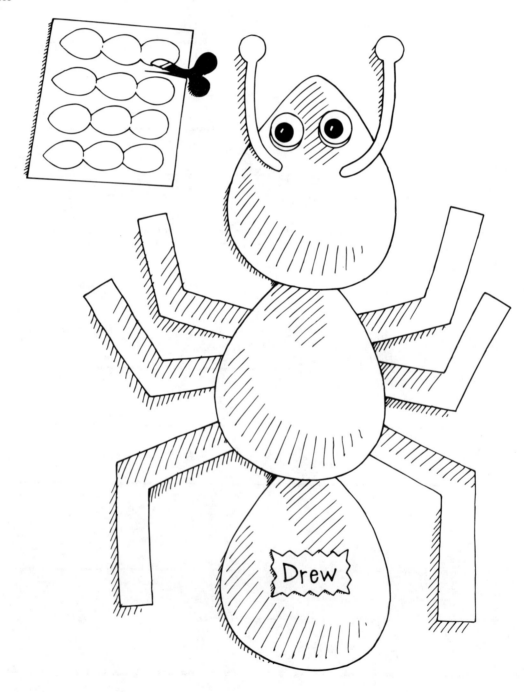

Kindness to All

_____ Ant said, " _____

_____

_____ . "

_____ Ant said, " _____

_____

_____ . "

_____ Ant said, " _____

_____

_____ . "

Culminating Event and Extra Fun

At the end of your unit, host a Bug Bonanza. Invite children and their families to visit the classroom so children can act as a guide to show off all the projects they completed during the unit and share the information they learned about bugs. Arrange your classroom so all the projects children completed are displayed. Prior to the event, have children practice leading a partner or small group around the classroom and explaining each project. This will help prepare children and make them feel confident when their family visits the classroom. Invite children to complete the following fun activities to provide decorations and props for the "big event."

Bugs in a Bottle Invitation

MATERIALS

✓ Bug Bonanza Invitation (page 61)
✓ green crinkled paper
✓ empty plastic water bottles (1 for each child)
✓ plastic bugs

Give each child a Bug Bonanza Invitation to complete. Have each child put green crinkled paper in an empty plastic water bottle. Invite children to add a few plastic bugs to the bottle. Tell them to roll up their invitation, place it inside the bottle, and take their bottle home to share with family members.

Beautiful Butterflies

MATERIALS

✓ *Waiting for Wings* by Lois Ehlert
✓ 6" (15 cm) tissue paper squares
✓ clothespins
✓ pipe cleaners
✓ close-up photo of each child's face
✓ art supplies

Read aloud *Waiting for Wings*. Discuss the life cycle of a butterfly. Invite children to choose two colors of tissue paper squares. Have them put the lighter color on top and use markers to add a dot pattern to the tissue paper. Have children grasp their two pieces of tissue paper inside a clothespin and glue them to the clothespin. Then, invite children to glue pipe cleaner antennae to the top of their clothespin. Glue each child's photo on the top of the clothespin as the butterfly's face. Invite children to decorate the body with glitter glue. Display the butterflies in your classroom.

Spider Bulletin Board Graph

MATERIALS

✓ *Miss Spider's Tea Party* by David Kirk
✓ Teacup reproducible (page 62)
✓ tagboard
✓ black butcher paper
✓ silver glitter
✓ construction paper
✓ 4 juices (different colors)
✓ plastic cups
✓ sentence strips
✓ art supplies

Copy the Teacup reproducible on tagboard, and cut out the cups to make patterns for children to trace. Paint a large white spiderweb on black butcher paper. Add silver glitter for a sparkling web. Draw a large Miss Spider on yellow construction paper, and cut it out. Accordion-fold black construction paper legs, and attach them to her body. Display Miss Spider and the web on a bulletin board. Cut out four construction paper pitchers to represent "spider tea." Make an orange pitcher for "butterfly tea," a green pitcher for "beetle tea," a purple pitcher for "cricket tea," and a pink pitcher for "caterpillar tea" (or use the colors of the "tea" children will be tasting). Write the corresponding color on each pitcher. Attach the pitchers across the bottom of the web to make a bar graph.

Read aloud *Miss Spider's Tea Party*. Pour the four juices into plastic cups, and invite children to participate in a "tea party" by tasting different types of "tea" (juice). After children have sampled all the flavors, invite them to choose their favorite. Have children trace a teacup pattern on construction paper that is the same color as their favorite tea. Then, have them cut it out and decorate it. Invite children to staple their teacup over the pitcher on the graph that is the same color as the tea they liked the most. Write at the top of the graph *Miss Spider had us for tea! What was our favorite? Look and see!* Invite children to analyze the graph. Use interactive writing to have children record their responses (e.g., *6 people liked beetle tea. Pink is the color of the favorite tea*) on sentence strips. Attach children's sentences to the graph. For extra fun, have children sit on a tablecloth on the carpet and use a tea set to make it seem like a real tea party. Remind children to hold their pinky out as they sip their tea! (You can use the "glyph bugs" from the activity on page 46 to hold the teacups on the graph.)

Bug Treats

MATERIALS

✓ Lovely Ladybugs Recipe (page 63)

✓ Bug Salad Recipe (page 64)

Gather for each child the ingredients and materials listed on a recipe. Give each child a copy of the recipe. For the Lovely Ladybugs recipe, mix red food coloring into the white frosting prior to the activity. Have children follow the recipe and color each illustration. For the Bug Salad recipe, have children write a number in each blank and then cut apart the directions. Tell them to staple the pages together to make a book. Then, have children put the ingredients into a small bowl, mix them together, and eat their tasty salad. Then, invite children to draw on each page how many "bugs" they put in the bowl. (To challenge children, invite them to add up how many bugs they ate.)

Bug Box Café

MATERIALS

✓ cardboard appliance box or premade playhouse

✓ tulle

✓ hot-glue gun

✓ plastic bugs

✓ plastic tea set and plastic foods

Build a cardboard playhouse from an appliance box, or use one you already have in your classroom. Drape tulle over the playhouse to give it a "bug box" appearance. Hot-glue plastic bugs to the tulle. Set up a tea party inside the playhouse with a plastic tea set and plastic foods. For extra fun, add menus, and have children think of "buggy" beverages such as Beetle Juice, Centipede Cider, and Caterpillar Cola to serve and drink.

Flyswatter Reading Sticks

MATERIALS

✓ flyswatters

✓ plastic bugs (optional)

✓ chopsticks or dowels (optional)

Cut out the center of flyswatters. Invite children to "read the room" with a flyswatter. Tell children to find a word or letter in the classroom and swat it with the flyswatter so it is showing through the center hole of the flyswatter. You can also have children use the flyswatter as they read Big Books to focus on individual words. Another way to have children get excited about reading is to hot-glue plastic bugs to chopsticks or dowels to create reading sticks.

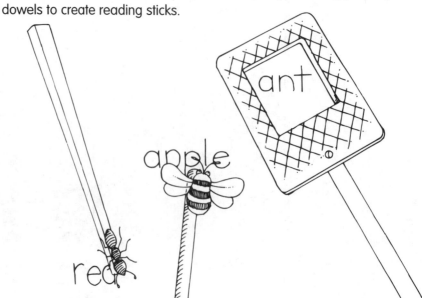

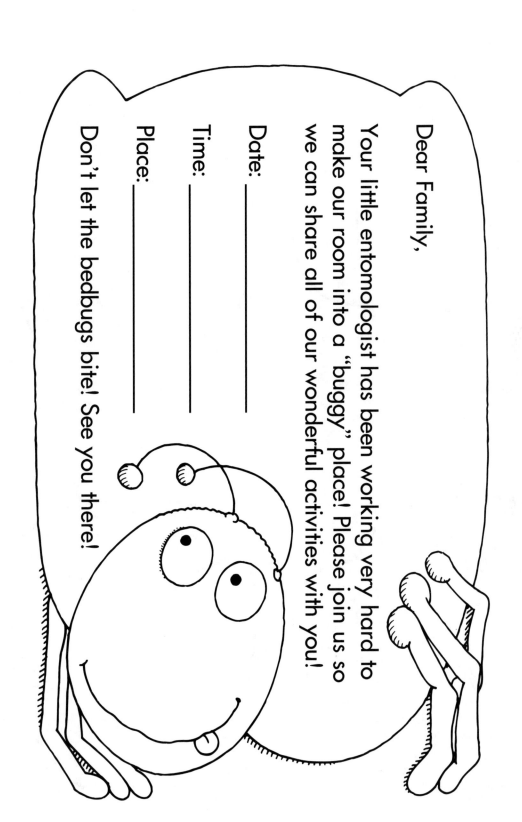

Dear Family,

Your little entomologist has been working very hard to make our room into a "buggy" place! Please join us so we can share all of our wonderful activities with you!

Date: _____

Time: _____

Place: _____

Don't let the bedbugs bite! See you there!

Teacup

Lovely Ladybugs Recipe

by Chef _____

Ingredients: red food coloring, vanilla frosting, round chocolate wafer, chocolate chips, M&M's® Minis

Materials: plastic knife, napkin

1 Start with a chocolate wafer.

2 Spread on red frosting.

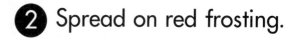
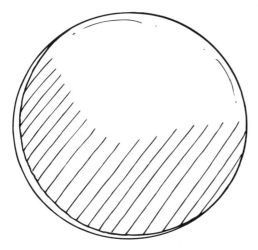

3 Add chocolate chip spots.

4 Use M&M's for eyes.

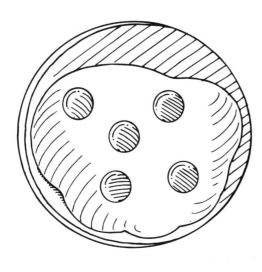
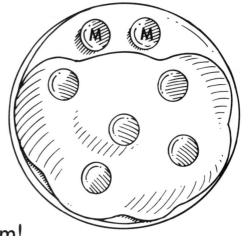

Yum! Yum!

Bug Salad Recipe

by Chef _____

Ingredients: raisins, Golden Crisp® cereal, Chinese noodles, chocolate chips, Froot Loops® cereal, Cocoa Puffs® cereal

Materials: small plastic or paper bowl, large spoon

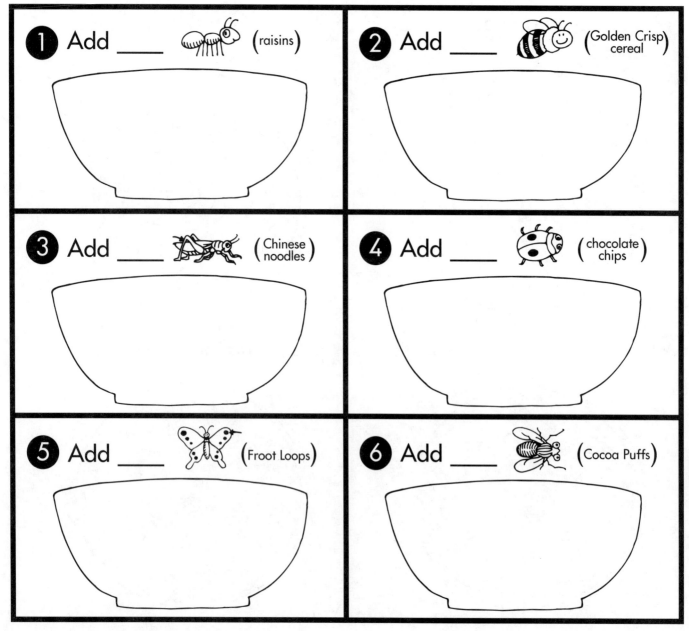

❶ Add ____ (raisins)

❷ Add ____ (Golden Crisp cereal)

❸ Add ____ (Chinese noodles)

❹ Add ____ (chocolate chips)

❺ Add ____ (Froot Loops)

❻ Add ____ (Cocoa Puffs)